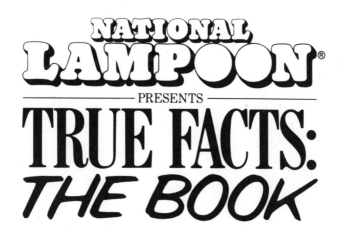

NATIONAL LAMPOON®

PRESENTS

TRUE FACTS:
THE BOOK

COMPILED BY JOHN BENDEL

CB

CONTEMPORARY
BOOKS

CHICAGO

Library of Congress Cataloging-in-Publication Data

National lampoon presents true facts : the book / compiled by John
    Bendel.
          p.   cm.
        ISBN 0-8092-4006-8 (pbk.) : $7.95
        1. Curiosities and wonders.   I. Bendel, John.   II. National
lampoon.   III. Title: True facts.
    AG243.N32   1991
    031.02—dc20   90-27789
                                                            CIP

Cover and interior design by Carolyn Hopp.

Front cover photo contributed by Michael Frank. Back cover photos contributed by R. E. Miller II (right) and Herm
Albright (left); clipping and headline contributed by James Little and Matt Bolch respectively.

Published by Contemporary Books, Inc.
180 North Michigan Avenue, Chicago, Illinois 60601
Manufactured in the United States of America
International Standard Book Number: 0-8092-4006-8

For Müf, Stinky, and the Boog

Contents

Report from the Editor

Over the years, stalwart readers of *National Lampoon* have submitted a wealth of material to a regular feature called True Facts. Some are so noteworthy, we decided they deserved to be in a book. This is it.

What is a True Fact? It is a grain of absurd glory for the man or woman who clipped it from a newspaper, tore it from a magazine, took a picture of it, carved it on a tree, etched it in stone, wrote it in the sand, shouted it to the heavens, or whistled it on the wind. In other words, it's an odd, often ironic, yet always genuine example of real-life funny stuff.

True Facts can include news stories, headlines, ads, photos—almost any item that can be clipped, copied, photographed, borrowed, bought, or otherwise acquired and sent through the mail. Most True Facts are unintentionally funny, but, yes, a few are obviously premeditated gags. That's because we're not trying to preserve some kind of conceptual purity here. We're just trying to have a good time.

Every item in this collection was submitted by the individuals credited. Those individuals are heroes and heroines all, for without them, there would be no True Facts, I wouldn't have this great job, and you would now be reading some inferior, far more expensive, and much less satisfying book.

If you care to join the anointed ranks of True Facts contributors (the choicest group of contributors known to humankind or anyone else), then by all means do. If we use your item, you will be forever enshrined in the glorious annals of *National Lampoon* history. We'll send you a free T-shirt, too. Please send your True Facts contributions to:

True Facts
c/o *National Lampoon*
155 Avenue of the Americas
New York, NY 10013

Be sure to include your T-shirt size, and watch for your item (and your name) in the very next issue of *National Lampoon*. If it's not in there, check the issue after that—you never know when it might appear.

By the way, because of the volume of mail, we disregard all submissions on rock, wood, wind, or the wings of angels.

Oh, and don't fill your envelope with tinsel glitter as Ken H. Lamb of Corvallis, Oregon, did. The stuff spilled all over the sofa, my wife got mad, and I had to blame it on the kids.

But now, please turn the page and take a look at some of the best True Facts ever to appear in print. Thank you.

John Bendel

Signs of Life

From the Random Monument Department

ON THIS SITE
IN 1897 NOTHING
HAPPENED.

Photo contributed by Gene Sorkin

. . . and the service will start as soon as He comes out.

Photo contributed by Mike Sellers

Jet-Propelled?

Photo contributed by Terry Hollis

She can hardly wait.

Photo contributed by
Virgil Rossner

Photo contributed by
Michael Landau

Photo contributed by Nicole Parsons

Picnic Hell

Photo contributed by Brian Weaver

Photo contributed by Chris Kidd

Name That Hole

Photo contributed by D. J. Hartley

Photo contributed by David Ferrall

Photo contributed by Pete Markay

Little Enigmas, Part I

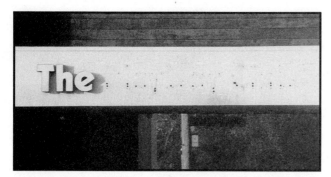

Photo contributed by J. Brown

Photo contributed by Mark Pauga

Actually, the dogs aren't all that bad.

Photo contributed by Karen Lee

Well, not all *that* new.

Photo contributed by
Theodore S. Bowes

A politician by any other name . . .

Photo contributed by Rob Culbertson

Zoogz Knows His People

Photo contributed by George Smith

The New Math

The Gramercy Arts Trio
Beautiful music for memorable moments

Weddings • Receptions • Parties

Flute • Violin • Cello & Vocalist

Ad from *New Jersey Monthly* magazine;
contributed by Al Evans

Dine With

Chris Demo Gus George

THREE BROTHERS RESTAURANT

Business card contributed by Ralph Gates

Quick! Into the shelter! Here come the customers!

Photo contributed by Corey Anderson

It's right next door to Big Al's 24-Hour Cathedral.

Photo contributed by Charles Shannon

Dream Boats

Photo contributed by Jim McLaughlin

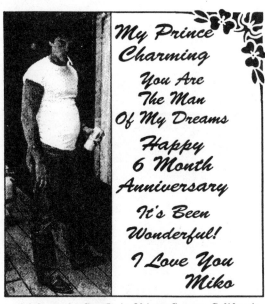

Ad from the San Luis Obispo County, California, *Telegram-Tribune*; contributed by Paul Velardi

16

Fast Food

WHIZ - AWAY FARMS

MILK · EGGS · GROCERIES · BEER · WINE

AT LOW PRICES

Photo contributed by Steve Bouchard

Peach pits, apple cores, and banana peels to your left.

Photo contributed by Karen Lee

And the kids don't look so swell either.

Photo contributed by Chris Gutscher

Kids Over the Hill

**ADULT
CHILDREN**

Photo contributed by Denis Navarro

Photo contributed by Oswald F. Angst

Photo contributed by Michael Frank

The swings are OK, but the slide is rough on the catheter.

RESERVED
FOR THE
AGED
AND
HANDICAPPED

Photo contributed by John Talbott

Our Mission: Clothing the Hungry and Feeding the Naked

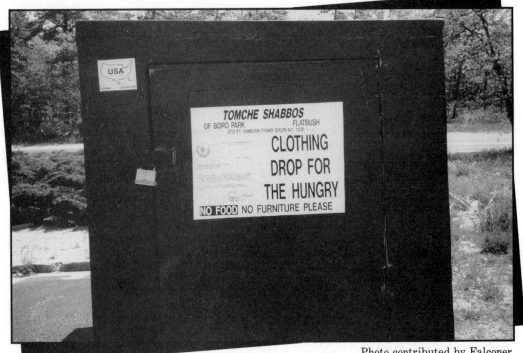

Photo contributed by Falconer

Oh sure, then heart problems will run for office, too.

Photo contributed by Bob Harrigan

For the closest thing to vegetables, it's . . .

Photo contributed by Nancy and David Berman

Even with a busted fin they still bite.

Photo contributed by S. J. Peters

Wimps Out for Minnows

Photo contributed by John O'Callaghan

The lights on their hats distract the bartender.

Photo contributed by
Lewis R. Harper

From the Truth in Advertising Department, Part I

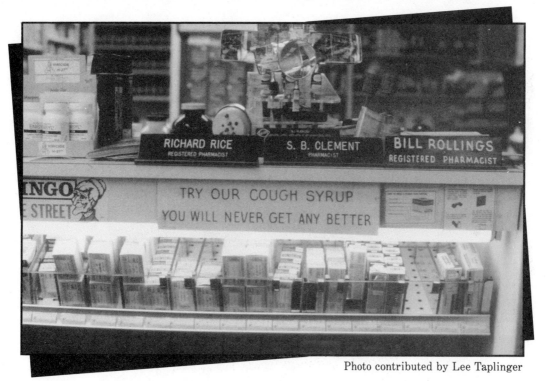

Photo contributed by Lee Taplinger

Praise the Lord and pass the peanuts.

Photo contributed by Philippe Meilleur

Swell Places to Eat and Sleep

Photo contributed by R. MacRae

Photo contributed by Steven and Wendy Schauder

Did you want hot sauce on that doctorate?

Photo contributed by Oswald F. Angst

The Better Part of Valor

Photo contributed by Oswald F. Angst

You'll be the first to know.

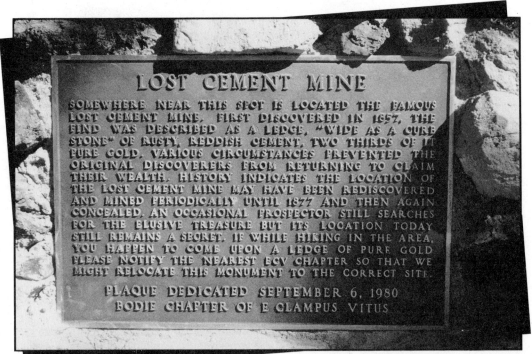

LOST CEMENT MINE

SOMEWHERE NEAR THIS SPOT IS LOCATED THE FAMOUS LOST CEMENT MINE. FIRST DISCOVERED IN 1857, THE FIND WAS DESCRIBED AS A LEDGE, "WIDE AS A CURB STONE" OF RUSTY, REDDISH CEMENT, TWO THIRDS OF IT PURE GOLD. VARIOUS CIRCUMSTANCES PREVENTED THE ORIGINAL DISCOVERERS FROM RETURNING TO CLAIM THEIR WEALTH. HISTORY INDICATES THE LOCATION OF THE LOST CEMENT MINE MAY HAVE BEEN REDISCOVERED AND MINED PERIODICALLY UNTIL 1877 AND THEN AGAIN CONCEALED. AN OCCASIONAL PROSPECTOR STILL SEARCHES FOR THE ELUSIVE TREASURE BUT ITS LOCATION TODAY STILL REMAINS A SECRET. IF WHILE HIKING IN THE AREA, YOU HAPPEN TO COME UPON A LEDGE OF PURE GOLD PLEASE NOTIFY THE NEAREST ECV CHAPTER SO THAT WE MIGHT RELOCATE THIS MONUMENT TO THE CORRECT SITE.

PLAQUE DEDICATED SEPTEMBER 6, 1980
BODIE CHAPTER OF E CLAMPUS VITUS

Photo contributed by Tom R. Porter III

News You
Can Abuse

Let's keep it on the ground, please, people.

Ozone Threatens Safe Sex

From the *San Francisco Chronicle*;
contributed by Bill Horgos

Hey, somebody could get killed in there!

Missouri Gas Chamber Is Unsafe

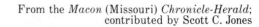

From the *Macon* (Missouri) *Chronicle-Herald*;
contributed by Scott C. Jones

And it took a lot of nerve, too.

Big bucks bagged by Balls

Calvin Balls, left, and Doug Ball, right, show off their *fine prizes, early Monday morning, at the Couch Cowboy Resort. There were a lot of deer reported this year and as Calvin said "It was like Dieppe out there."*

From the *Wiarton* (Ontario) *Echo*; contributed by Roly Thomas

From the Authentic Bogus Headline Department

Fake Bogus passes suspected

At least two people are apparently circulating phony ski passes for Bogus Basin Recreation Area, according to the Boise County sheriff's office.

Boise County officials confirmed Saturday that they are investigating a case involving at least two suspects and an unknown quantity of phony passes.

They said no further information would be released until the 2-week-old investigation is completed.

Bogus Basin Marketing Director Jane Dechambeau said ski area personnel found some suspicious passes and turned them over to the sheriff's office for investigation.

From the *Idaho Journal*; contributed by T. Tiersch

It's too noisy around here, sonny. We'll take ours to go.

No such thing as a free lunch

When planning your summer musical activities, kindly take care to read the fine print. Summerfest officials report that when the Madison folk rock band Free Hot Lunch appeared there last year, several senior citizens misread the calendar and mistakenly figured they were in for free chow. Though their songs are spicy, the band has nothing to do with food.

From the *Milwaukee Journal*; contributed by Greg Reske

She died with her pants on.

Cotton briefs

Cotton friends regretted to hear of the death Tuesday of Mrs. Mattie Lou Nix of Camilla.

From the *Pelham* (Florida) *Journal*; contributed by Christopher Ellrich

Who wants a congressman named Tou Tou anyway?

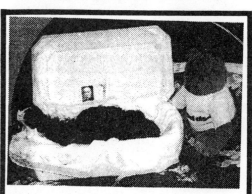

In memory of my best friend, Tou Tou who passed away April 17, 1989.
After 15 years of travelling all over the country with me I sure miss you dear friend.
I know you are up there in heaven.
If they decide to send you back, come back as you were, a beautiful little dog, not as a human being because they may make a mistake and send you back as a dirty, rotten, greedy, back-stabbing liar.
Rest in Peace Tou Tou
Herman and Tiger

From the *Moncton* (New Brunswick, Canada) *Times Transcript*; contributed by R. Matthew

From the Which Way Is Up Department

Age of wisdom

Researchers at the University of Wales College in Cardiff are to spend two years trying to discover whether old people are really wiser than the young. A £65,000 project funded by the Economic and Social Research Council starts next year but the psychologists say they have to define what wisdom is first.

From the London *Daily Telegraph*;
contributed by Len Walker

Okay, so we all had a rotten day.

Seacoast Scorecard

Football

By *The* Associated Press
American Conference

East	W	L	T	Pct.	PF	PA
Buffalo	0	0	0	.000	00	00
Indianapolis	0	0	0	.000	00	00
Miami	0	0	0	.000	00	00
New England	0	0	0	.000	00	00
N.Y. Jets	0	0	0	.000	00	00
Central						
Cincinnati	0	0	0	.000	00	00
Cleveland	0	0	0	.000	00	00
Houston	0	0	0	.000	00	00
Pittsburgh	0	0	0	.000	00	00
West						
Denver	0	0	0	.000	00	00
Kansas City	0	0	0	.000	00	00
L.A. Raiders	0	0	0	.000	00	00
San Diego	0	0	0	.000	00	00
Seattle	0	0	0	.000	00	00

National Conference

East	W	L	T	Pct.	PF	PA
Dallas	0	0	0	.000	00	00
N.Y. Giants	0	0	0	.000	00	00
Philadelphia	0	0	0	.000	00	00
St. Louis	0	0	0	.000	00	00
Washington	0	0	0	.000	00	00
Central						
Chicago	0	0	0	.000	00	00
Detroit	0	0	0	.000	00	00
Green Bay	0	0	0	.000	00	00
Minnesota	0	0	0	.000	00	00
Tampa Bay	0	0	0	.000	00	00
West						
Atlanta	0	0	0	.000	00	00
L.A. Rams	0	0	0	.000	00	00
New Orleans	0	0	0	.000	00	00
San Francisco	0	0	0	.000	00	00

Score table from the *Portsmouth (New Hampshire) Herald*;
contributed by Gary Petersen

Popes in Retirement

Photo contributed by David Bateman

And it's hell on spelling, too.

Study: Long-term marijuana use harms mermory

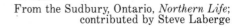

From the Northhampton, Massachusetts, *Daily Hampshire Gazette*;
contributed by Jennifer L. Hoey

Newborn Babies Survive Murder Attempt by Distracted Editor!

Death Notices

GIRLS
• to Lee Ann and Colin Bell of Dowling, Monday, Jan. 5.
• to Leslie and Fred Stanford of Sudbury, Monday, Jan. 5.

• To Carol and David Fowler of Coniston, Saturday, Jan. 10.

BOYS
• to Jeanne and John Courtney of Sudbury, Sunday, Jan. 4.

• to Vivian and Bruce Greer of Sudbury, Tuesday, Jan. 6.
• to Cindy and Jim Meisenheimer of Sudbury, Tuesday, Jan. 6.

From the Sudbury, Ontario, *Northern Life*;
contributed by Steve Laberge

Colon outburst highlights trial

BOSTON — In an outburst during the second day of his U.S. District Court trial on narcotics trafficking charges, a Fitchburg man leaped to his feet and shouted denials of government claims that he operated a cocaine distribution operation from his Worcester convenience store.

"I no sell drugs!" cried 37-year-old Rafael Colon of 14 Pleasant St., Fitchburg as court officers hurried to restrain him.

From the *Fitchburg* (Massachusetts) *Sentinel & Enterprise*; contributed by Bruce Siart

Boner rises, shines after inauguration gala

From the *Nashville Banner*; contributed by Matt Bolch

Venereal disease is linked to crack

From the *Altoona* (Pennsylvania) *Mirror*; contributed by Denis Navarro

Men picky about noses

From the *New Orleans Times-Picayune*; contributed by Susan D. Indest

From the Out of the Frying Pan Department

Steer Runs Away From Packing Plant, Enters Steak House

Associated Press

Omaha

A hulking Angus steer broke out of a cattle pen at a packing plant yesterday and crashed into the front doors of one of the city's best-known steak houses.

"He was excited and half-crazed, and I said to myself, 'I don't want that guy in here,'" said Tom Kawa, president and part-owner of Johnny's Cafe, who encountered the steer. "We would have had a hell of a rodeo."

From the *San Francisco Chronicle*; contributed by Dennis Senft

. . . and the deer can hardly wait.

Deer Hunters Balls are scheduled

There will be a number of Deer Hunters Balls on Friday in the area, including those at Pardners on Lake Buchanan, Hard Times on Hwy. 281 south of Marble Falls and at Ed's River palace on Hwy. 281 between Johnson City and Marble Falls.

At Parnders, the Deer Hunters Ball will run all night with 50-cent drinks for the ladies until 10 p.m. and "the best DJ in the Highland Lakes area!"

At Hard Times, the Deer Hunters Ball will run 8 p.m. until midnight with the band, "River City Rounders." There is a $3 cover charge. Call 825-3285 for reservations.

From the *Burnet* (Texas) *Bulletin*; contributed by Jamie Marmolejo

. . . and after we nab 'em, we squash 'em with this here roller.

The Delta police department is in the middle of its Spring CounterAttack program, but that doesn't mean it's turning a blind eye to other offences. Here, police officers use a radar gun to nab speeding motorists.

From the *Delta* (British Columbia) *Optimist*; contributed by Gordon Felotick

Just don't wash the dog in it.

Peculiar water safe to drink

Boiling order lifted by state

PECULIAR — Residents can once again drink from their water faucets without fear.

The Missouri Department of Natural Resources lifted an order suggesting that Peculiar residents boil water for five minutes before drinking it. The DNR placed the boil order Thursday, after a vehicle struck a fire hydrant, knocking the hydrant loose.

"The boil order is off and everything is all right," said Ray England, utility superintendent of Peculiar.

From the *Belton* (Missouri) *Star-Herald*; contributed by Julia Hylander

... and it didn't look so great on TV either.

Bloody butt hurts Ramirez

Chavez still unbeaten in 62 pro fights

From the *Lahaina* (Hawaii) *News*;
contributed by D. Hunter Bishop

It's a Wonderful Day in the Neighborhood

● A 64-year-old on the 1100 block of Santa Fe Avenue reported that when he left his house at 8:15 a.m. April 5 his windows were clean and when he returned at 11 a.m. they were dirty.

He said his next-door neighbor, a 66-year-old woman, had spit on them. He claimed to have photos of her spitting on his windows in the past.

The neighbor called him a bastard and said she spits on his windows only when he throws things on her roof. The officer saw window stained and also saw refuse on the woman's roof. The man said he only throws things on her roof after she throws things in his backyard.

From the
San Diego (California) *Tribune*;
contributed by Lisa Pasqua

● AN ITALIAN who had been injured in a traffic accident was placed on a stretcher which rolled out the back of an ambulance that was rushing him to a hospital in Avellino. On reaching the hospital, the driver discovered his patient was no longer in the vehicle. The patient hitchhiked the rest of the way to the hospital and was treated for his injuries.

From the Albany, California, *Journal*;
contributed by Mary Thomson

At 9 p.m., a Oak Harbor resident reported his neighbor has been placing his dog on the hood of his car and driving approximately 70 m.p.h. The neighbor told the complainant the dog loved it.

From the *Whidbey News-Times*,
Oak Harbor, Washington;
contributed by Ritchard W. Brown

To hospital — Longview police took a 41-year-old Longview man to St. John's Medical Center for mental health assistance Sunday after it was reported he was behaving strangely at his home on 17th Avenue. Police were told he had washed himself with motor oil and cleaned his trailer with tomato juice Sunday.

From the Longview, Washington, *Daily News*; contributed by Darren Day

Signs of Life, Part II:

Let's Go for a Drive

Just Do It

Photo contributed by
Mr. and Mrs. Jack A. Rye

Little Enigmas, Part II

Photo contributed by Regina K. Carter

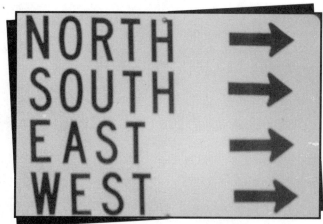

Photo contributed by Lindsay Henderson

The Tooth Fairy Goes Corporate

Photo contributed by Edward Callary

From the Truth in Advertising Department, Part II

Some crack-ups are better than others.

Photo contributed by Lorraine Rowe

Photo contributed by Mike Straub

**. . . and there's a penalty
for early withdrawal.**

**OK, all you dead people,
let's move it.**

- Photo contributed by Kurt G. Hagdorn

Photo contributed by Scott Mulligan

Banal byways

Photo contributed by Patricia Murdock

Photo contributed by Alan Barr

Photo contributed by Paul Cote

Just in case you're driving a 747.

Photo contributed by Joseph L. Gazza

That's odd—Rover was in the yard just a minute ago.

Where to Find the Nimblest Dink in the County

Photo contributed by Jim Muellerleile

Yeah, it's really somethin' to see, but the mist smells like ammonia.

Photo contributed by Jerry Labb

A Car with a Mission

Photo contributed by James Thomson

They'll slide right off your bumper.

Photo contributed by
Jim Motter

Okay, but remember: no touching.

Photo contributed by
David R. Selden

Honest, officer, I tried to sotp but I didn't know how.

Photo contributed by N. Leed

Just Buy It

Dogs have gotten stupider since the sixties.

Wednesday, April 21, 1965

132 CLASSIFIED DISPLAY   132 CLASSIFIED DISPLAY

WANTED

DOG

Male Preferred

Must be of Collie strain and be
able to lip-read and be bilingual.

Apply:

BOX 9395,
CHRONICLE-HERALD

From a 1965 issue of the *Chronicle-Herald*;
contributed by Laura Robinson
and Mike Thompson

From the Well-Endowed Rabbit Department

From a craft supply catalog;
contributed by Art Mares

And next month, corned beef and cabbage pizza!

Photo contributed by Trevor J. Baker

Please Disregard the Zombies

From an unidentified Kansas newspaper; contributed by Gina Meyer

Nice Work If You Can Get It

DICK WORKER
Hiring now
Only Fee $65/Adv. Licensed Job
Info. Agency. Job Times, Inc.

From *The Columbus* (Ohio) *Dispatch*;
contributed by Gerald Kilbane

Just slap it on the counter and we'll see what we can do.

Cocks Repaired: Grandfather, mantle, cuckoo, etc. Bill Mosher.   x

---

From the *Henrietta* (New York) *Shopper-Journal*;
contributed by Peter M. Gramiak

From the Friendly Greeting/Fond Farewell Department

The
Leonard Memorial Home Ltd.

| 565 Duane St. | 0S033 Church St. | 3S532 Batavia Rd. |
| Glen Ellyn | Winfield | Warrenville |

Changed Your Lifestyle?
Call Welcome Wagon

When you change your lifestyle, your needs are changing, too. Welcome Wagon® can help you find services that meet your requirements.

My basket of gifts and information are all absolutely *FREE*. Millions of Americans contact us...engaged women, new parents, and new citizens. Have you changed your lifestyle or know someone else who has? Call me:

Kathleen Culp
Nancy Johansen

If you live in my neighborhood, I'll be happy to visit you. If you reside elsewhere, I'll refer you to another Representative. If no one is available in your area, you may be interested in the position yourself. I'll forward your request for employment information to our Memphis, Tennessee office.

Side-by-side ads in the *Glen Ellyn* (Illinois) *News*; contributed by Patrick J. Carmody

Sounds like the school needs a root canal.

Ad from the *Miami Beach Sun-Reporter*; contributed by Mary Jane Newborn

Please don't eat 'em in public.

A product label; contributed by Lorin Wegand

From the Who Wouldn't Department

Will swop tire ashtray collection for land in Maine, Vermont, or New Hampshire. M 731 NY

From *Yankee Magazine*;
contributed by Ken Brinnick

Take the A train.

PREGNANCY information. Free pregnancy tests. Confidential. On subway.

Ad from the *Toronto Sun*;
contributed by Debbie Czarnuch

Cadmium found in livers of lobsters from L.I. Sound

NEW LONDON (AP) — The state Department of Health Services is considering issuing a health advisory against eating the livers of lobsters taken from eastern Long Island Sound after samples of the green organs showed elevated levels of cadmium, a department official said Wednesday.

"We haven't issued an official advisory at this time, but when people call us up and ask us, we tell them they can reduce their exposure to PCBs and cadmium by not eating the hepatopancreas," said Bob Toal, chief of the department's toxic hazards section.

YOU DESERVE THE BEST!

Caplan's
WALLINGFORD'S OWN SUPERMARKET

THURS., FRI. & SAT. SPECIAL

LIVE LOBSTERS
$3.99 Lb.
1¼ LB. AVERAGE

ARRIVING 12 NOON - Thurs., Fri. & Sat.
NO PHONE ORDERS • WHILE SUPPLIES LAST EACH DAY

Not responsible for typographical errors. We reserve the right to limit quantities.

Side by side in the Meriden, Connecticut, *Record-Journal*; contributed by Brian T. Lampher

Wanted: Warm Individual With Dressing

HI out there! I'm a young at heart lady, 49. Some things I enjoy are people, life, being honest & sincere, dining & dancing, quiet evenings, nature, laughing, family and friends movies, music, my job & some sports. If you are a man that enjoys similar things, I would like to eat you. So drop me a line to Herald Box CH1905.

From the *Calgary* (Alberta) *Herald*;
contributed by Mike Benton

He's a great catch, mom, except for one little flaw.

FORMER forester, vegetarian, 32 yr. old male, 3 degrees, seeking understanding and compassionate friend for occasional outings to all star wrestling. Reply to Box JP915 The Edmonton Journal.

From the *Edmonton* (Alberta) *Journal*;
contributed by Ryan Cromb

Dave the pet needs a pal.

... and the summer will be a LuLu.

PETS/LIVESTOCK

●*WHITE MALE, ATTRAC-TIVE*, 6'2'', 38, fun loving, af-fectionate, many interests, desires to meet like female, 23-28 for friend. Write to: Dave, ████████ (Send photo). (PE4-2)

From an unidentified
California newspaper;
contributed by Mary Pyle

'Companions'

A cute male named Boo Boo seeks female named Woo Woo for a special summer.

Ad from an unidentified
Canadian newspaper;
contributed by Jarett Sherman

Don't ask what it tastes like.

Product label from East Germany; contributed by Larry Kinner

Now! Assholes wherever you want them! Automatically!

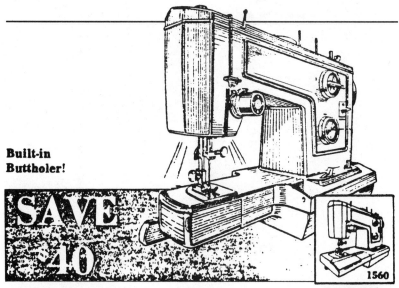

Built-in Buttholer!

SAVE $10

1560

From the *Kansas City Star*; contributed by Paul S. Imlay

Does Fido clash with your new decor?

We Now Paint Dogs!

$2.00 OFF

COMPLETE GROOMING

New Clients Only Please
Expires September 30, 1987

Specializing In The Grooming
Of Your Dog And Cat

Offering:
Hot Oil Treatments • Flea Shampoos
Nail Trimmings • Shampoo & Trims

FOR
PET'S SAKE

111 West Main • Carmel

From the *Carmel* (Indiana) *Highflyer*;
contributed by Mark E. Rogers

Photo contributed by
Ronald R. Kyser

Bring your blemishes, and let's get down!

**MEDICAL ASSISTANT/RE-
CEPTIONIST** Party time for
dermatology practice. Drexel Hill
location.

From the *Jerusalem Post*;
contributed by Beth Pfeffer

Watch out for the lady with the whip in the funhouse.

Amusement-park ride ticket;
contributed by Gary R. Winders

... and we'll gobble a while.

> If you were the lady in the Greyhound Grocery Friday, June 3:
> About 3:30, your 3-year-old was crying a little and my daughter was talking to her and said she was a little turkey like I was.
> **Call me at** ▮▮▮▮▮▮

Ad from the Jeffersonville, Indiana, *Evening News*; contributed by Angela Carpenter

How many times have I told you not to let your body go off by itself?

Century 300 Car Seat

39⁹⁹
REG. 49.99

Has 5 point harness design and extra padding for safety and comfort.

From the *Providence* (Rhode Island) *Sunday Journal*; contributed by Steve Browner

PASS-N-WIND MOTEL

Pt. Salubrious, Chaumont, NY

NEW · MODERN
REASONABLE
6 UNITS
ELECTRIC HEAT · T.V.

From a promotional brochure;
contributed by Bill Woods

You might consider a face-lift, too.

That explains the powder burns on Blitzen.

Losing Hair???

Before   After

THE Drug-Free Alternative

(Distributorships Available)

From *New Life*;
contributed by Brian B. McColgan

Ad from an unidentified newspaper;
contributed by Jon L. Johnson

Your kitchen's been strangled and your bedroom's been shot.
Trust me, ma'am, you don't want to go in there.

Your Home Has Been Exterminated

PREFERRED PEST CONTROL
1127 Dean Forest Road
Savannah, Georgia 31405

DATE _____

Notice left in a Savannah, Georgia, apartment;
contributed by Larry D. Vincent

And it turned her life upside down.

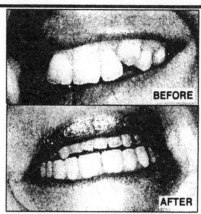

THIS PATIENT
ACHIEVED A
BEAUTIFUL
SMILE
THROUGH
ADULT
COSMETIC
TOOTH
MOVEMENT

**Treatment time:
3 months**

BEFORE

AFTER

J. Charles Culbreath, D.D.S.
General Dentist
2008 Cloverdale Ave., Winston-Salem

From the *Winston-Salem* (North Carolina) *Sentinel*;
contributed by Harold Johnson

Just follow those scratching guys.

Creighton University
Dept. of Dermatology
is looking for

volunteers with

JOCK ITCH

for a short study of a new
topical drug treatment

All treatment is provided *FREE* of charge

Confidential inquiries to:

Mon.-Fri. 8:00-4:30

From the *Omaha World-Herald*;
contributed by Ron Dufek

Been sitting on a toadstool?

GENITAL WART VOLUNTEERS
NEEDED

FOR INVESTIGATIONAL RE-
SEARCH TRIAL USING INTERFER-
ON. TREATMENT AND LAB WORK
FREE. FOR MORE INFORMATION
CALL MONDAY-FRIDAY (9-4 pm)

NORTHERN VIRGINIA
BOARD CERTIFIED INFECTIOUS DISEASES

From the *Washington Post*;
contributed by Leigh Anna Ramstad

Big Sale at the Ook Store

**SALE
20% Off
All
Cookooks**

Coupons not valid on sale books
Good through 7-15-88

**Little Professor
Book Center**

Ahwatukee Mercado

From the *Ahwatukee* (Arizona) *News*;
contributed by Mary Riege Laner

Career of the Year

...and it doesn't hurt to be stupid, too.

8:30 am to 5:30 pm

Telemarketing

ALLIGATORS

I'm interested in hiring 3 semi-obnoxious, pushy people for a very boring, repetitious job of telemarketing. My current staff is the laziest group of individuals that you will ever see, drag themselves to work Mon-Fri. to decide whether to complain about the coffee, weather, the thermostat or the Manager! When that's over, somehow they manage to organize themselves, make their calls and make lots of money. Which is surprising because no one wants to buy anything we sell! Because the price is too high and the economy stinks.

From the *Kansas City Star*; contributed by F. Dorsey Luchok

7 TOUGH GUYS NEEDED To box against inmates in a Federal Prison. Will train, prize money to all applicants. No boxing exp. please.

From the Vancouver, British Columbia, *Province*; contributed by Caroline Vesely

From the Some Ingredients Are Better Left a Secret Department

Don't Miss Our 1st Annual

Road Kill Chili Supper

Friday, Oct. 20 at 5 p.m.
Kremmling Town Square

Sponsored by
Kremmling Area Chamber of Commerce

From the Granby, Colorado, *Sky-Hi News*; contributed by Leo V. Piechocki

And you can live in the cinders when we're done.

WANTED:
Dead or Alive
*A House To Burn**
Badger Road Area

The North Star Volunteer Fire Department needs a house to burn for training.

Help clean up your neighborhood. Impress your friends and neighbors. Donate your house, shack, shed or mobile home.

CALL TODAY
*NOTE: Donor must own property.

From the *Fairbanks* (Alaska) *Daily News-Miner;*
contributed by Robert Vigue

My old pair had me plugged up good.

From the Houston *Yellow Pages*; contributed by Terry Collins

And mazeltov to you, Mr. Wiggly!

From an unidentified Alabama newspaper;
contributed by Katie Dye

Signs of Life, Part III:

It's Showtime!

Loud, Libidinous Videos

Photo contributed by
Warren Couvillon, Jr.

Hi-ho, Loni!

7:30 **5** **Evening** Take a test ride in the newest ride in Disneyland; Loni Anderson.
8:00 **4** **Movie** ★★ *The Impostor* (1984) Anthony Geary, Lorna Patterson. A con artist charms his way into the principal's post at a Midwestern high school and

From the *Seattle Post-Intelligencer*;
contributed by Jeff Swanson

OK, who snuck the guy in here?

From the Pittsburgh edition of
TV Guide;
contributed by Lou Pappa

If you want a decent IQ, it's a buck and a half.

Photo contributed by Gerry Evans

Bring earplugs.

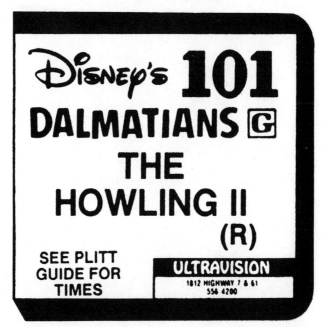

From the *Charleston* (South Carolina) *News & Courier*;
contributed by J. Tatum

I never did trust those Fly Gods.

Photo contributed by Hans and Mitch

The worse it is, the more they like it in Philly.

From the *Philadelphia Daily News*;
contributed by Mark Johnson

. . . and it goes in the potty.

CHANNEL 4

6.0   **THE CHANNEL FOUR DAILY.**
9.25   **THE ART OF LANDSCAPE.**
11.0   **AS IT HAPPENS,** at London Zoo.
12.0   **THE PARLIAMENT PROGRAMME.**
12.30   **BUSINESS DAILY,** with Susannah Simons.

1.0   **SESAME STREET:** The letters are S and H and the number is 2.

2.0   **POWERBASE (T)** (rpt.).
2.30   **THE MEASURE OF SUCCESS:** Saving.

From an unidentified European newspaper;
contributed by James Little

I Do, I Do,
But . . .

I do, I do, but don't stand too close, okay?

Long-Cox

Shannon Marie Cox and Mark Edward Long were married Aug. 30, 1989, at Graceland Wedding Chapel, Las Vegas, Nev.

The bride is the daughter of Dale Cox Jr. of North Aurora and the late Pamela Cox. The groom is the son of Janet Grady of Punta Gorda, Fla., and John Long of Aurora.

The bride is a 1988 graduate of West Aurora High School. She is employed by Farmers Insurance Group. The groom is a 1982 graduate of East Aurora High School. He is employed by Berry Bearing Co.

They live in Aurora.

Mr. and Mrs. Long

From the Aurora, Illinois, *Beacon-News*; contributed by Jack Schultz

I do, I do, but I have here a list of fifteen card-carrying Communists in this very wedding!

Joseph-McCarthy

Michelle Carolyn Joseph of Sierra Madre and Sean Robert McCarthy of Pasadena are planning a June wedding. She is the daughter of Mrs. Carrie Joseph of Sierra Madre, and the granddaughter of Mr. and Mrs. William Mann of Whittier. McCarthy is the son of Mr. and Mrs. Dennis McCarthy of Pasadena.

The prospective bride attended Westridge School in Pasadena, and is now a senior studying speech pathology at Cal State Northridge. Her fiance attended La Salle High School in Pasadena and received a degree in English from UCLA. He teaches social studies and

MICHELLE JOSEPH and SEAN McCARTHY

English as a Second Language in the Los Angeles Unified School District.

From the Pasadena, California, *Star News*; contributed by Travis Kelly

I do, I do, but shouldn't we have boots and an umbrella?

Storm-Flood

Mr. and Mrs. Wallace Storm of Birmingham have announced the engagement of their daughter Pamela to William Flood, son of Donald Flood of Novi and Barbara Flood of Naples, Fla.

The bride-elect is a graduate of Andover High School and is employed as a marketing coordinator at the Thomas A. Duke Co.

Her fiance is a graduate of Farmington High School and is employed as a complex supervisor for Village Green Management Co. Both attended Ferris State University.

A late March wedding is planned at the First United Methodist Chuch of Birmingham.

From an unidentified Michigan newspaper; contributed by Alan Valentine

I do, I do, but I should hope so, big fella.

Ball-You

Sophia You, daughter of Mr. and Mrs. Yong Su You of Seoul, South Korea, and Maj. Randall N. Ball, son of Mr. and Mrs. Billy C. Ball of St. Albans, were married May 12 at the Yongsan Military Installation in Seoul.

From the
Charleston (West Virginia) *Gazette*;
contributed by Joe Freeman

I do, I do, but please, don't let go.

Cox-Held

Married June 10 at St. Joseph's Catholic Church were Angie M. Cox, Marion, and Rick H. Held, Orlando, Fla. The Rev. John McDermott performed the 2 p.m. ceremony. A reception for 200 guests followed at Longbranch Supper Club.

From the *Cedar Rapids* (Iowa) *Gazette*;
contributed by Bill Irwin

I do, I do, but did we have to get married at the ballpark?

Beers, Franks

Lewis Beers of King of Prussia, Pa., and Mrs. Richard Foust of Roland Park in Baltimore have announced the engagement of their daughter, Elizabeth Skeath Beers, to Thomas Stone Franks, son of Mr. and Mrs. Robert Franks of Annapolis.

A graduate of West Chester University, Miss Beers is the director of athletics at Oldfields School in Glencoe.

Mr. Franks, a graduate of St. Mary's College, is corporate computer training coordinator for Provar in Towson.

A spring wedding is planned.

ELIZABETH S. BEERS
and THOMAS S. FRANKS

From the *Washington Post*; contributed by Chris Nugent

I do, I do, but couldn't we have potatoes for a change?

Brown-Rice

Ormond Beach Memorial Gardens was the setting June 3 for the wedding of Patricia Ann Rice and Michael Scott Brown, with the Rev. Frederick Frustch officiating.

From the *Daytona Beach* (Florida) *News Journal*; contributed by Gary Demianycs

I do, I do, but then I'd say we were made for each other, wouldn't you?

Kuntz-Dick

Lisa Renee Kuntz and Gary Wayne Dick plan to be married in a 12:30 p.m. ceremony July 14 at Carmel United Methodist Church in Carmel, Ind.

From the *Evansville* (Indiana) *Press*; contributed by Gavito Solis

I do, I do, but keep your hands to yourself 'til after the reception.

BUNN-GRABS

KING — Ashley Elizabeth Grabs of King and Kevin Brett Bunn of Raleigh were married Saturday at King Moravian Church.

The bride is the daughter of Mr. and Mrs. Omnie Omily Grabs Jr. of King. Parents of the bridegroom are Mr. and Mrs. Franklin Bunn of Raleigh.

Bunn

After a reception at King Recreation Acres, the couple left on their wedding trip to Florida. They will live in Raleigh.

From the Raleigh, North Carolina, *News and Observer*; contributed by Mike Sellers

I do, I do, but good garter belts are hard to find.

Stock-King

The marriage of Miss Gail Elaine King and Mr. Frederick Joseph Stock III was solemnized Sept. 2 at St. Louis Cathedral. The bride is a daughter of Mr. and Mrs. Franklin Theodore King and the bridegroom is a son of the late Mr. Stock Jr. and the late Mrs. Jenny Marie Avella Stock. The Rev. Ray Wilhelm, O.M.I., officiated at the ceremony, which was followed by a reception at the Windsor Court Hotel.

From the *New Orleans Times-Picayune*; contributed by Bonnie LeBlanc

I do, I do, I *must* say!

Martin-Short

Lisa Rae Short, daughter of Mr. and Mrs. Raymond C. Short of Perry Hall, and Stephen Andrew Martin, son of Mr. and Mrs. Joseph A. Martin of Kingsville, were married Oct. 15 in the Loyola College Chapel.

Stephanie Short and Joseph Martin Jr. were honor attendants.

Both Mr. and Mrs. Martin are graduates of Loyola College. She is a master's candidate at the University of Baltimore. He is a CPA with Wooden & Benson.

Mrs. Stephen Martin

From the *Baltimore Sun*; contributed by Nancy Thayer

I do, I do, but someone just stole our Yugo.

Good-Loser

Mary Ellen Good of Hummelstown, daughter of Mr. and Mrs. Thomas T. Good of Sutton Avenue, Hopwood, became the bride of Stephen T. Loser, son of Mr. and Mrs. Thomas J. Loser of Hershey on July 1 at St. Joan of Arc Church in Hershey.

The Rev. John Hoke officiated at the service.

Given in marriage by her father, the bride wore a full length blush satin brocade gown with ballgown neckline and sleeves, basque waistline and chapel length train. A veil of illusion fell from a satin headpiece of roses and pearls.

MR., MRS. LOSER

From the *Uniontown* (Pennsylvania) *Herald-Standard*; contributed by Mike Skoda

I do, I do, but who are all those short guys?

Snow-White

Immaculate Conception Catholic Church provided the setting Feb. 10 for the wedding of Anne Elizabeth Snow and Danny Lee White, both of Cedar Rapids. The 2 p.m. ceremony was performed by the Rev. Phillip Schmitt.

From the *Cedar Rapids* (Iowa) *Gazette*; contributed by Janet Gagne

I do, I do, but who's gonna walk Dino?

FLINT-STONE

CAMBRIDGE — Mr. and Mrs. Wayne S. Flint of Cambridge and Mr. and Mrs. Carl Lewis of New Britain, Conn., announce the engagement of their daughter, Bonnie Lynn, of Barre to Timmy Carol Stone, the son of Mr. and Mrs. William Stone of Barre and the late Karlene H. Stone. The bride-to-be is a 1985 graduate of Montpelier High School. She is employed as a customer service representative at the Granite Bank. Her fiance attended Spaulding High School. He is a mechanic at Stone's Service Station. A May 19, 1990, wedding is planned.

From the *Rutland* (Vermont) *Herald*; contributed by Derek Yesman

Signs of Life, Part IV

Eat and Get Out

Where to Find the Best-Fed Trucks in America

Photo contributed by Billy Cox

Not at the table, please.

FATHER'S DAY
at the
Oyster Reef

**SPECIAL! Prime Rib or Filet Steak
& Cajun Prawns . . . PLUS Complimentary
Glass of Champagne and a "Hooker"
for Dad!
Casual Dining Over The Water - 11:30 am to 10 pm**

10th Avenue & EMBARCADERO OAKLAND

From the *Oakland* (California) *Tribune*; contributed by Bill Hoch

We boiled 'em, and now they're mad.

Photo contributed by Michael P. Morgan

Restaurant or rest stop?

Notice: Seating Limited When Chef Excited

Photo contributed by Craig MacFarland

Photo contributed by William Stage

The Original BAR·B·QUE
BROIL YOURSELF ON YOUR OWN TABLE

Photo contributed by Margaret von Biesen

**No shoes, no shirt,
no cummerbund, no service.**

Heavy on the studs, hold the spats!

Photo contributed by Chris Gutscher

Photo contributed by
Richard Terrill

Come Be the Main Course

Sandwich Field
Light Drink & Salad
Nice Eat You ?

Photo contributed by Scott Kuhlman

Hey, can you guys do "Feelings"?

THE SINGING NUNS OF ST. CECELIA'S CHORALE

APPEARING AT MISTER C'S STEAKHOUSE

Mon. — July 15 — Shows At 7-8 & 9 P.M.
Tues. — July 16 — Shows At 6-7 & 8 P.M.
(NO COVER CHARGE)
Make Your Reservations Early

MISTER C's STEAKHOUSE
5319 No. 30th St.

From an unidentified Nebraska newspaper;
contributed by Mariclaire Fleming

119

Aberrant Burgers

Photo contributed by Clark Kidd

Photo contributed by George Smith

Photo contributed by Ron Mayers

Just don't expect Giancarlo Giannini.

Photo contributed by Guy Major

Here's your hat; what's your hurry?

Photo contributed by Carl G. Jacobson

Why Kids Shouldn't Read

Photo contributed by Herm Albright

Separate Seating or Catch Your Own?

Photo contributed by Bob Ring and Lynn Ruby

Yum.

Anonymous photo contribution

Photo contributed by Timothy Harnett

125

Photo contributed by Judi Rogers

Because you said you were tired of McDonald's, that's why.

Photo contributed by G. D. Young

126

. . . and a side order of Lysol, please.

Photo contributed by Rory Peterson

Swim and Party with Your Supper

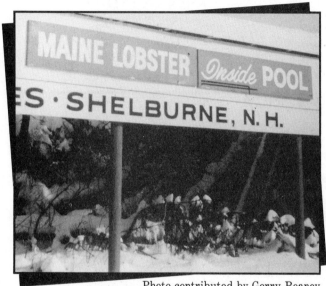

Photo contributed by Gerry Beaney

You Should See 'Em Dance

Photo contributed by J. Rowley

128

Do you have any idea how hard it is to kill one of those things?

Photo contributed by Mike Ruplinger

Remember to duck when she turns around.

Photo contributed by Lou Carlson

Tales from
the Crypt

From the Do Unto Others as Was Done Unto You Department

Photo contributed by Greg Blair

. . . but not quick enough.

Look, I got here as soon as I could.

Photo contributed by Randy Palmer

Photo contributed by Lee Taplinger

The Old Hot Dog Burial Ground

Photo contributed by John F. Ybarbo

Wrap 'Em Tight And Send 'Em Parcel Post

Ad from *The Baptist Record*; contributed by Walter H. McDonald

Frankly, Kent, from the condition of the bodies, it must have been Superman.

Photo contributed by John J. Frongillo

R.I.P., a Great Bandstand American

Photo contributed by Brad Irons

. . . and we'll always remember you for your, well, you know.

Photo contributed
by Christopher Clyde

... but not for long.

Photo contributed
by Herm Albright

Don't worry, boss, I buried it where no one will ever guess.

Photo contributed by Herm Albright

You just can't keep a *bon homme* down.

Photo contributed by Paul Sutherland

Last Stop for Roger Rabbit

Photo contributed by
Zach Thompson

Signs of Life,
Part V:
Risky Business

Who Named the Business?

DOO DOO FASHION

Photo contributed by John Mayer

FROZEN CORPSE RANCH

Photo contributed by Josh Williams

144

**Fresh! From Chernobyl
Dairies, it's . . .**

**You can't wear them, but take
our word for it: they're really clean.**

Photo contributed by Ranger Bob

Photo contributed by Greg Gattuso

Shoot the Piano Player

Photo contributed by
Daniel K. Purlsey

Lighting from Hell

LAMP HADES

Photo contributed by
Daniel C. McHugh

Car Dealers Without Pants

Photo contributed by Jerry T. Wilson

Photo contributed by David E. Holubitsky

I'd say about $54 million, not including the bleachers.

Photo contributed
by Steve Thomas

I'll take a dozen, uppercase please.

Photo contributed by Tom and Beth Gould

I know you're busy, Lord, but could you please clean my rug?

Photo contributed by Ron Chase

See the Lady in Net Stockings for Details

Photo contributed by Douglas A. Danke

. . . a division of Thank You, Ma'am, Inc.

Photo contributed by Vint Davis

. . . for Sexy Mouse and Duck Wear

Photo contributed by Shaun Ivory

From the guys who brought you cement boots . . .

Photo contributed by Charles Gary Peterson

Do you take 'em away, or do I have to bring 'em over?

Photo contributed by Bill Lynch

Your prices are good. Your store is great. In fact, there's only one thing I'd change, Mr. Dumfart.

Photo contributed by Dale Fundling

We forget about the hard part, and pass the savings on to you!

Photo contributed by Linda Peterson

Don't call us, we'll call you, unless the damned thing doesn't **work again,**
in which case you'd better call us **after all.**

Photo contributed by Richard Carter

Watch out for the tongue prints on the wash.

Photo contributed by Danny Wallace

If you're looking for commitment, try the hardware store.

Photo contributed by Bert Prestridge

Dancing Derrières

Photo contributed by
Gale Gardner

Burgeoning Business

Photo contributed by
B. L. LaCoyne

Sure, just after I paid full price.

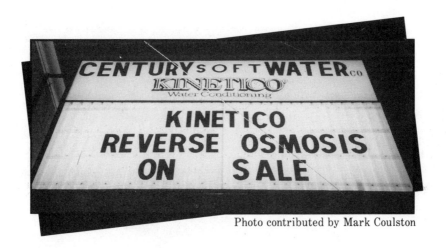

Photo contributed by Mark Coulston

Employment for the Frustrated

Photos contributed by Thomas J. Ferri

When it absolutely, positively has to get there . . .

Photo contributed by Robert Stevenson

... with the most convincing sales force north of the border.

Photo contributed by Greg Swanson

A bucket of killies or some dame in fishnet stockings?

Photo contributed
by Greg Lawrence

. . . Featuring the Famous Gesundheit Coffee Shop

Photo contributed
by Mary Campbell

**So a weimaraner ate your poodle?
You want to make something of it?**

**Gimme a mermaid
and caption it "Woof."**

Photo contributed by David R. Hiller

Photo contributed by Lance K. Trask

166

Go ahead. Squeeze an udder. Kick a hoof. She's as good as new.

Photo contributed by Mark R. Youtzy

Don't miss the big swizzle stick sale.

Photo contributed by Gord Kurbis

Mr. Cox and Mr. Cox are tied up, but Mr. Cox will see you.

Photo contributed by Michael Paston

New, Used, and Rebuilt

Photo contributed by Richard Carter

Photo contributed by Rick Kneidel

Photo contributed by S. Veres

Please bring your own anesthetic.

SURGERY
Dr.A.G.N.LAKHA
Mon-Sat-9.30-11.30am
Mon-Fri-4.00-6.00pm
Closed Wednesday Evening
Tel-L.V.718711

28A

McCULLOCH
CHAIN SAWS

Photo contributed by David Jolles

A John by Any Other Name

Photo contributed by
Michael Johnson

Photo contributed by
Gary Tillotson

Photo contributed by Louisa Beal

Keep It Clean

Photo contributed by Jon Krassenstein

Well, almost anyway.

Photo contributed by Keith Benkery

If you like the movie, you'll love the industry.

Photo contributed by Robert Stanek

Colossal Sales

Photo contributed by Jim Mantel

Photo contributed by Phil Steffen

Photo contributed by Jack Marshall

. . . and heaven is a quieter place.

Photo contributed
by R. E. Miller II

Bring your own potato chips.

Photo contributed by
Michael Frank

Hunting's More Fun When You're Plowed

Photo contributed by
Will Veber